ROALD DAHL

Beastly Brutes & Heroic Human Beans

Illustrated by
Quentin Blake

Written by
Stella Caldwell

Welcome

THIS IS A WELBECK CHILDREN'S BOOK

Published in the United States in 2020 by Welbeck Children's Books, an imprint of Welbeck Children's Limited, part of Welbeck Publishing Group, 20 Mortimer Street London W1T 3JW

First published by Carlton Books Limited in 2019.

ISBN: 978-1-83935-012-2

Printed in June 2020 in Heshan, China.

10 9 8 7 6 5 4 3 2 1

Managing Art Editor: Matt Drew
Executive Editor: Bryony Davies
Cover Designer: Deborah Vickers
Production: Nicola Davey

Well done you! By buying this book, you've helped another child. 10% of all Roald Dahl income* goes to our charity partners.

* All author payments and royalty income net of third party commissions. The Roald Dahl Charitable Trust is a registered UK charity (no. 1119330).

WELBECK

This is no ordinary book...

Press out any areas with wavy lines like these to make the pages into exciting shapes, peep through to see surprises, and open doors

...it's a press-out paper adventure!

To press out your pieces, hold the page steady with one hand, and use your other hand to press gently on the edges of the shape and remove the extra paper. Most of this spare paper can be recycled.

But you'll also find characters inside that you can press out and keep, just like Charlie and Willy Wonka below. Go on, have a go now—press them out!

Press out areas that are surrounded with dashed lines like these—they are your characters to keep

You can store your figures in the envelope on the last page

Now it's time to get started!
What are you waiting for?

Charlie
and the
Chocolate Factory

PROUDLY PRESENTING:

Charlie Bucket
Your chocolate-loving guide

Grandpa Joe
Charlie's young-at-heart grandfather

Mr. Willy Wonka
The greatest magician the world
has ever known

Augustus Gloop
A boy so fat, he looks like he's been
blown up by a pump

Violet Beauregarde
The world's No. 1 gumchewer

Veruca Salt
A very rich peanut-factory heiress

Mike Teavee
A boy who just loves to watch television

Charlie Bucket

I'm Charlie, and I'm VERY pleased to meet you! As soon as I'm old enough, I'll be the owner of Willy Wonka's chocolate factory.

Mother and Father

But when this story began, my family—all seven of us—lived squashed up together in a tiny, two-room house. My father worked hard, but there was never enough money. How I hated the horrible empty feeling I got in my tummy from never having enough to eat!

I LOATHE CABBAGE . . . BUT ABSOLUTELY **ADORE** CHOCOLATE!

Grandpa Joe

HE'S TALL AND BONY—AND **96 AND A HALF** YEARS OLD.

The oldest of my four grandparents, Grandpa Joe loves to tell stories. He was the one who told me all about Mr. Wonka's marvellous inventions, and the tiny, shadowy people behind the windows of his factory.

And it was Grandpa Joe who believed I could find a golden ticket, and who gave me his last coin to buy a chocolate bar.

Grandpa Joe hadn't been out of bed for years, but when I found my ticket, he leaped up and DID A JIG.

Grandma Josephine

Grandpa George

Grandma Georgina

The Chocolate Factory

I USED TO WALK PAST THE FACTORY'S **HUGE GATES** AND SNIFF THE AIR.

OPEN ME!

Mr. Wonka's factory once had thousands of workers. But then spies started stealing his secrets, so he had to get rid of them all! The factory was deserted for months. Then, one day, the chimneys started smoking again. But nobody ever went in . . . or came out.

WHEN WE STEPPED INSIDE, THE FIRST THINGS I NOTICED WERE THE **SMELLS . . .**

ROASTING COFFEE

MELTING CHOCOLATE

AND BURNED SUGAR

The Chocolate River

The place is like a rabbit warren inside: passages lead in EVERY possible direction. The most important room of all is called The Chocolate Room. I've never seen ANYTHING like it.

A huge river of melted chocolate flows right through it. And everything is edible, from the grass and the trees to the pink hard-candy boat that is Willy Wonka's private yacht!

Willy Wonka

Who else could make ice cream that never melts, cavity-filling caramels, or invisible chocolate bars for eating in class? The man is a genius!

If I had to say what animal he reminded me of, it would be a squirrel: it's the way he cocks his head and darts around. You get the feeling there is nothing he misses!

THE GENIUS HIMSELF

Top hat

Plum velvet tailcoat

Pearly gray gloves

Bottle-green trousers

WHEN GRANDPA JOE SAID WILLY WONKA WAS A **MAGICIAN**, HE WAS RIGHT!

The Oompa-Loompas

"THERE ARE NO SUCH PEOPLE!" I SAID.

I didn't believe Grandpa Joe when he told me about the tiny people at Wonka's factory. But now I've seen them with my own eyes!

Marvelous workers

They love to dance and sing

Rather mischievous!

Mr. Wonka told us he first met the Oompa-Loompas in Loompaland, a dreadful place full of hornswogglers and whangdoodles. They were so petrified, they were living in tree houses and eating caterpillars!

But then he discovered the poor Oompa-Loompas longed for cacao beans, so that settled it. He shipped all of them to his factory, and they couldn't be happier!

Augustus Gloop

Fast facts

Hobby: eating
Appearance: face quite like a ball of dough (frankly, looks like he's been blown up by a powerful pump)

Augustus's hobby is eating

When I first saw Augustus, I was struck by the sheer SIZE of him. He is enormous. Though I suppose that should be WAS—he's as thin as a straw since the chocolate river pipe incident!

Augustus was never going to last long on Willy Wonka's tour, and as it was, he fell at the very first hurdle.

HIS MOTHER SAYS SHE'D RATHER HE WAS EATING THAN RUNNING AROUND LIKE A HOOLIGAN.

Augustus told us his mouth was watering like crazy the minute we stepped inside the factory. The smells! But it was the river that must have gotten to him. All that chocolate—enough to fill every bathtub in the land, Mr. Wonka said.

HE JUST
HAD
TO TASTE IT!

He ended up lying down and lapping it up. And then he just sort of . . . rolled in.

Just imagine what it must have been like for Augustus getting sucked up the pipe and hearing his mother screech, "Come out of there at once!"

HE
BLASTED
UP THE TUBE
LIKE
A ROCKET!

Violet Beauregarde

Fast facts

Hobby: champion gum chewer
Appearance: powerful jaws
Most likely to say: Just so long as it's gum . . .

Champion jaws

When I heard that Violet had been chewing a piece of gum for THREE MONTHS SOLID, it did turn my stomach a little. Grandma Josephine called her a beastly girl!

Grandma Georgina thought that Violet would come to a sticky end. And if turning into a blueberry is a sticky end, then she was probably right . . .

CHOCOLATE'S ALL RIGHT, BUT IT'S **GUM** SHE ADORES.

The Great
Gum Machine

When Mr. Wonka told us about his new invention—gum that was breakfast, lunch, and supper—Violet didn't lose any time in helping herself to a piece.

He may have said it wasn't quite ready, but she didn't think he was being serious. But then she started swelling up . . .

To the
Juicing Room!

I BET BEING PURPLE IS NO FUN AT ALL!

Veruca Salt

Veruca has every luxury money could buy—and she isn't even a tiny bit grateful!

THE OOMPA-LOOMPAS CALLED HER A LITTLE **BRUTE!**

She only has to lie on the floor screaming for something, and her parents get it for her. That's how she ended up with a golden ticket.

Grandma Georgina said she needed a good spanking—but perhaps being thrown down the nut room garbage chute was worse than that!

The Great Glass Elevator

Imagine an elevator that can take you directly anywhere—sideways, longways, slantways—at the press of a button. That's how the craziest elevator I've ever seen works!

You have to hold on to one of the ceiling straps, because the elevator jumps away at the speed of a rocket. Swerving and lurching, it shoots upward and drops like a stone, twisting and turning, faster and faster …

IT'S A **MILLION** TIMES BETTER THAN A ROLLER COASTER!

Mike Teavee

MIKE
REQUIRES
COMPLETE
SILENCE
TO WATCH TV.

18 toy pistols
strapped to
his body

Grandma Georgina thought Mike Teavee was an undeserving little brat. But I suppose by the end of the tour he really WAS pretty little!

If I'm honest, Mike seemed pretty bored by the factory. So when he saw the words TELEVISION CHOCOLATE, he didn't even ask. He just pressed the elevator button.

MIKE WASN'T MORE THAN AN INCH TALL.

Mrs. Teavee wasn't too pleased at the sight of her tiny son

When Mr. Wonka showed us a chocolate bar being sent by TV, Mike got pretty excited. I bet he was thinking, "Why not me?"

He didn't seem to mind when he came out tiny—he was the first person ever to be sent by television AND he could still watch it!

Then his mother insisted on getting him stretched out, and he ended up 10 feet tall! But worst of all for Mike, his father swore he would throw out the TV the second they got home.

The chocolate bar, before shrinking

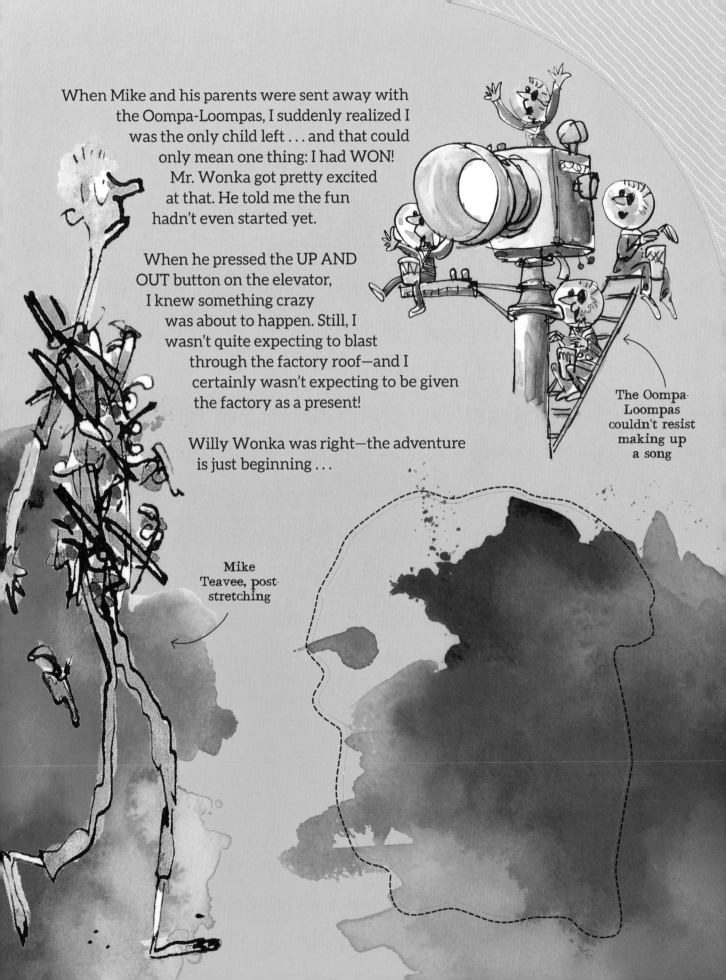

When Mike and his parents were sent away with the Oompa-Loompas, I suddenly realized I was the only child left . . . and that could only mean one thing: I had WON! Mr. Wonka got pretty excited at that. He told me the fun hadn't even started yet.

When he pressed the UP AND OUT button on the elevator, I knew something crazy was about to happen. Still, I wasn't quite expecting to blast through the factory roof—and I certainly wasn't expecting to be given the factory as a present!

Willy Wonka was right—the adventure is just beginning . . .

The Oompa-Loompas couldn't resist making up a song

Mike Teavee, post-stretching

The Twits

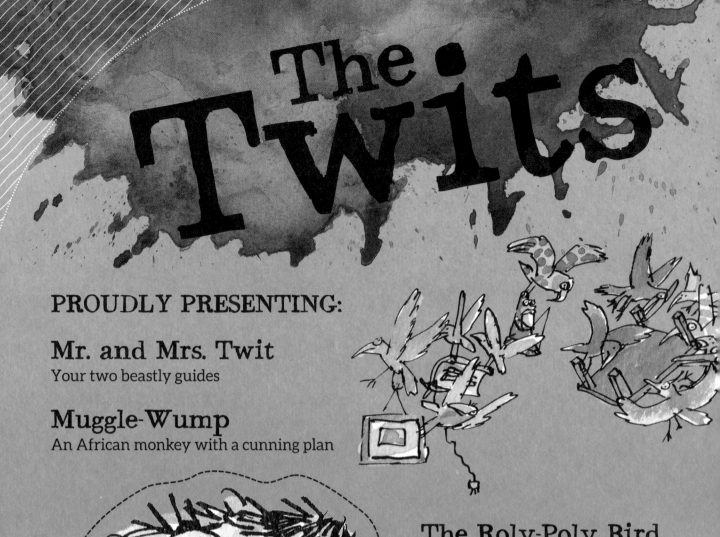

PROUDLY PRESENTING:

Mr. and Mrs. Twit
Your two beastly guides

Muggle-Wump
An African monkey with a cunning plan

The Roly-Poly Bird
A magnificent jungle bird with a fondness for travel

Mr. Twit

I'm not big on people who stick their noses into other people's business. Nasty, nosy people usually get what they deserve! But since you're here, being nosy, I suppose I'd better tell you something about me.

I'm proud to say I'm a twit. I was born a twit, I'm still a twit, and I'll remain a twit till the day I die! How's that for commitment?

I'M HORRID AND HATEFUL.

I don't have many pleasures in life, but these are the things that make life worth living:
- **Being hairy**
- **Being foul**
- **Bird Pie**

And last but not least:
- **Playing beastly tricks on my beastly wife!**

BRISTLY BEARDS

I'm not one to boast, but my hairy face is my crowning glory. There may be lots of men around with beards, but I don't just have a few straggly tufts. No, every part of my face—except for my forehead, eyes, and nose—is covered in a THICK, BRISTLY LAYER. The stuff even sprouts out of my ears and nostrils!

I LIKE TO THINK OF MY FACE AS A **HAIRY JUNGLE**.

Truly pathetic beards

MAGGOTY
GREEN CHEESE—
SCRUMPTIOUS!

Do you know what my secret is? I never wash my beard, not even on Sundays. (Actually, I never wash, period.) Food clings to the bristles, and that means I never go hungry.

A moldy cornflake

The slimy tail of a canned sardine

Ground chicken liver

If I'm feeling a bit hungry, all I have to do is slip out my tongue and go exploring—and I soon come across something tasty. My mouth is watering just at the thought of it!

Mrs. Twit

The best thing about the way I look is my glass eye. It's always looking the other way, and I can see how that gives people the shivers. And if I really want to give someone a fright, I just pop it out! Hee hee!

I was quite a catch when I was younger. People said I had a nice face. But what's the point of that? Who wants a face that shines like sunbeams? I'm nasty through and through, and I want people to know it!

I'VE GOT **MY EYE** ON YOU, SO DON'T YOU FORGET IT!

My looks have improved as I've got older

The Big
Dead Tree

Our
delightfully
landscaped
garden

Ready for
the pie!

ANY BIRD
WILL DO!

OUR HOUSE

When Mr. Twit and I built our house, our number-one concern was keeping nasty, nosy children OUT—so there isn't a SINGLE window in the place. And our yard is always choked up with stinging nettles.

The most important thing in our yard, though, is The Big Dead Tree, and let me tell you why. Every Wednesday, Mr. Twit and I have Bird Pie for supper—and how do you think we catch the birds?

The day before, Mr. Twit paints the tree's bare branches with HUGTIGHT, the stickiest glue in the world. And when the birds fly in to roost for the evening, they soon discover that they're stuck fast!

Bird Pie

HE'LL
BOIL US.
HE'LL
STEW US!

Imagine Mr. Twit's fury when, one Wednesday morning, he went out to collect the bird, and instead found four beastly BOYS stuck to the branches.

He couldn't wait to get his hands on the wretches, and he started climbing the tree. Then, just as Mr. Twit reached them, one wriggled out of his trousers and leaped down, and the rest followed suit— BARE BOTTOMS and all!

NOBODY DENIES
MR. TWIT HIS PIE
AND GETS AWAY
WITH IT—SO
WATCH OUT!

Mr. Twit's Trickery

Nothing gives me more pleasure than getting the better of Mrs. Twit. It takes enormous skill to carry out my beastly tricks.

WHAT A **GLORIOUS SIGHT!**

1. I once put a frog in my wife's bed. When she shrieked, I told her it was a Giant Skillywiggler with teeth like screwdrivers!

2. One night, I secretly stuck a tiny piece of wood to the bottom of her walking cane. I did this every night until one day she realized the cane was too long for her. She thought she was shrinking, and there's nothing worse than the DREADED SHRINKS!

3. If you're shrinking fast, you need to be stretched! Well, that's what I told Mrs. Twit ... With her feet tied to an iron ring and 100 balloons attached to her upper body, she really was stretched most marvelously.

Filling more balloons!

4. After her stretching, it was the simplest thing in the world to cut through the strings holding her down and release the old hag into the sky.

Mrs. Twit's Trickery

HERE I COME, MR. TWIT!

I can outdo that rotten turnip Mr. Twit with my tricks every time! How about the time I popped my glass eye into his beer mug? He sure did jump when he saw it staring up at him!

Then there was the time I mixed wriggling worms into his spaghetti. He didn't know he'd been eating worms until he'd swallowed EVERY last morsel. Hee hee!

He thought he had the better of me with the ballooning-up trick, but I bit through some of the balloon strings, and I was soon drifting gently down ...

There was nothing gentle about my arrival, though! I landed smack on top of him!

Squishy worms ... tricked again!

Muggle-Wump
(in his own words)

I live in a cage in Mr. and Mrs. Twit's yard with my family, and together we are . . .

THE GREAT UPSIDE-DOWN MONKEY CIRCUS!

How we dreamed of escaping back home to the African jungle!

And how we loathed seeing those poor birds getting stuck to The Big Dead Tree week after week. We tried to warn them, but they couldn't understand our language.

We had given up hope of ever escaping when one day we had a visitor, an old friend from the African jungle . . . It was none other than the Roly-Poly Bird!

WE REALLY **HATED** PERFORMING THOSE SILLY TRICKS.

Me

My wife

My children

The Roly-Poly Bird explains...

I may live in the African jungle, but I'm an extremely well-traveled bird. Air travel is usually an expensive business, but I can travel anywhere I want in the world and it's free!

When I visit a country, I ALWAYS learn the language. What's the use of being somewhere new and not knowing how to speak to others?

FLY AWAY, BIRDS, AS FAR AS YOU CAN . . .

I was so happy I could help the poor birds that were getting stuck on *The Big Dead Tree*. It was quite a challenge rhyming in a new language, but it worked!

. . . MR. TWIT IS NOT A NICE MAN!

UPSIDE DOWN

Mr. and Mrs. Twit were expecting to have the last word, but there's a problem, I'm afraid. They can't! Little did they realize their monkeys would play the best trick of all . . .

It all started when I stopped the birds from sitting on The Big Dead Tree and the Twits didn't get their Bird Pie. They didn't like that one bit.

THEN MUGGLE-WUMP HAD A SIMPLY **MARVELOUS** IDEA.

It really was quite simple to stick the entire contents of the Twits' living room on to the ceiling while they were out.

Rescued from the pie

All that standing on his head gave Muggle-Wump time to plot his revenge!

Muggle-Wump and his family built an amazing tree house at the top of a very tall tree

Of course, when the Twits returned, they thought they must be standing upside down—and that's why . . .

. . . they decided to stand on their HEADS.

Did I mention that just before, two ravens had kindly sprayed their heads with HUGTIGHT glue?

HELP!

The Twits wriggled and squirmed, and choggled and churned, but they became quite cemented to the floorboards. In fact, before long, their heads began to shrink into their necks, and their necks into their bodies . . .

Deliciously sticky glue

WE'VE GOT THE TERRIBLE...

Actually, I was wrong to say the Twits didn't have any last words. It's just that they're not quite the words they would have wanted.

S
H
R
I
N
K
S
!

Just clothes, shoes, and a walking cane left ... not to mention the glass eye

THE BFG

PROUDLY PRESENTING:

Sophie
Your brave guide

The Man-Eating Giants
Nine beastly brutes that guzzle human beans:

The Bloodbottler
The Fleshlumpeater
The Childchewer
The Bonecruncher
The Manhugger
The Meatdripper
The Maidmasher
The Gizzardgulper
The Butcher Boy

The BFG
A Big Friendly Giant with a fondness for sandals

The Queen of England
Also known as Her Majester

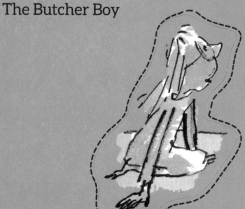

SOPHIE

TURNS OUT THE BFG IS NOTHING BUT A **GREAT BIG SOFTIE!**

His ears are just ENORMOUS

I'm Sophie, and I simply can't wait to introduce you to my dear friend the BFG ... not to mention the Queen of England! (It's not everyone who can count Her Majesty as a personal friend.)

But first things first: I'm an orphan, and when this story began, I was living at Mrs. Clonker's Orphanage. It's a dreadful place. If you break any of her silly rules, you're locked up in the cellar with the rats, and given nothing to eat for a day and a night!

I wear thick-lensed glasses—I'm almost blind without them!

I'm eight, and my mind never stops whirring

KIDSNATCHED

I'M NOT OFTEN FRIGHTENED, BUT I SCREAMED.

Even though I hated the orphanage, I can't say I was too thrilled when a giant hand simply plucked me out of bed. I mean, how would YOU feel?

It really was pretty terrifying. I was smothered in a blanket and carried through the night at a terrific speed. I fully expected the BFG to fry me like a slice of bacon for his breakfast.

On my way to Giant Country!

But if I've learned ANYTHING from this, it's not to judge people before you know them. Because the BFG is one of the loveliest beings you could ever hope to meet! In fact, he's my best friend.

THE BFG

Even if I was terrified when I first saw the BFG, I couldn't help being pretty impressed at the same time. Who ever saw a giant wearing sandals?

More peculiar was the way he squiffed and squiddled his words! He was impolite too—at one point he told me, "Your head is full of squashed flies!"

It turned out the BFG's jumbly way of talking is easy to understand once you get the hang of it.

Ucky mucky: messy

Babblement: conversation

Hopskotchy: marvelous

He's INCREDIBLY tall—24 feet at least

WHAT HE **MEANS** AND WHAT HE **SAYS** ARE TWO DIFFERENT THINGS!

When I first saw him, he was blowing a long trumpet through a neighbor's window

Silly-looking sandals. And his toes are as big as sausages!

SNOZZCUMBERS AND FROBSCOTTLE

MAGGOTWISE!

Because the BFG doesn't gobble human beans, he had to make do with snozzcumbers instead. And even though they look impressive, they're DISGUSTEROUS!

But the BFG's favorite drink, frobscottle, is simply delumptious. It tastes of vanilla, cream, and raspberries. You can feel the bubbles dancing around in your tummy!

ROTSOME!

REPULSANT!

SICKABLE!

DELUMPTIOUS!

The bubbles in frobscottle fizz downward rather than upward— and that leads to the best whizzpoppers ever! Bravo!

DREAMCATCHER

As I already mentioned, the BFG's ears are huge—but they can hear EVERY SINGLE TWIDDLY THING.

THE FARAWAY MUSIC OF THE STARS

LITTLE ANTS CHITTERING

THE SINGING OF SPIDERS

The BFG can even hear dreams. When a dream passes through the night air, it makes a soft hum that no human could ever hear.

Every morning, he used to travel to Dream Country to catch dreams and put them into bottles. And each night, when all the other giants were guzzling human beans, the BFG blew sweet dreams into the rooms of sleeping children.

THE BFG SAYS DREAMS ARE VERY **MYSTERIOUS** THINGS.

Rows and rows and rows of dreams in jars

DREAM COUNTRY

The eerie place where the BFG catches his dreams is completely flat with no trees. Everything seems gray and white. It's terribly cold, and there's not a sign of a living thing anywhere.

THERE'S A GHOSTLY MIST THAT SWIRLS AROUND YOUR HEAD.

There are many types of dreams, but these are some the BFG told me about:

Golden Phizzwizard: the best possible dream you can have

Winksquiffler: a pretty good dream

Bogthumper: a not-so-nice dream

Grobswitcher: a pretty scary dream

Trogglehumper: the very worst nightmare you can imagine! The trogglehumper I saw the BFG catch thrashed around in its jar as if it were in a rage!

Once a dream's been captured, it's no longer completely invisible

MAN-EATING GIANTS

I'll never forget my first sight of the nine beastly giants who lived alongside the BFG in Giant Country. It's the **COLOSSAL SIZE** of them that is really brain boggling—they are much bigger than the BFG. And they are all so ugly!

The BFG told me that every single night, in some part of the world, some poor human beans got eaten alive. Can you imagine anything more horrible?

Some of the giants' favorite places for catching tasty human beans:

Wales: they taste a little fishy

Chile: where the Chile beans are cold

Sweden: for a sweet-and-sour taste

Panama: they have a strong taste of hats

Jersey: a bit woolly but tasty all the same!

The BFG says he's the runt

Me flying
out of the
Bloodbottler's
mouth

IMAGINE BEING
TRAPPED IN A
BLACK CAVE WITH
THE STENCH OF
ROTTEN MEAT.

THE BLOODBOTTLER

Not everyone can say they've been in a giant's mouth and lived to tell the tale. But that's what happened to me when the Bloodbottler grabbed the snozzcumber that I was hiding in, and took a giant bite!

He really is a foul sight, with a squashed-up face, piggy eyes, and enormous frankfurter lips. His fingers are the size of tree trunks!

It's lucky for me the snozzcumber was so foul tasting that the Bloodbottler spat it—and me—out. Because one of his very favorite foods is little English school-chiddlers . . .

Fast asleep,
until . . .

. . . the BFG blew
a TERRIBLE
nightmare into
his ear

THE FLESHLUMPEATER

I IS GUZZLING
ALL HUMAN BEANS,
WHETHER THEY BE
HALF-BAKED BEANS
OR QUEEN BEANS . . .

He's hideous to look at with his meaty black tongue. But it's the way he snores that's REALLY disgusting. He makes a repulsive snorting noise, and bubbles of spit blow out of his lips and pop over his face. Ugh!

He's the biggest giant of all, but a terrible coward. He was thrashing around when the trogglehumper began to work—it turns out he's petrified of Jack in *Jack and the Beanstalk*!

And when I stuck the pin of the Queen's brooch into the Fleshlumpeater's ankle, you should have heard him SCREAM!

It was only a pinprick, but he thought a dreadly dangerous viper had bitten him!

SUPPER TIME

The man-eating giants mainly snatch human beans from their beds, but occasionally they use other cunning methods.

The **Gizzardgulper** lies high up between the roofs of city houses. When he sees a human bean, he simply reaches out and grabs it—a bit like a monkey taking a nut.

The **Meatdripper** disguises himself as a tree and waits for a family to settle down beneath his "branches" for a picnic. It's soon clear that it's the Meatdripper enjoying a picnic!

The **Butcher Boy** swims along the coast looking for sunbathers (the plumper, the better).

THE CHILDCHEWER:
feeds on juicy chiddlers

THE MAIDMASHER:
likes the ladies!

THE MANHUGGER:
has a wicked hug

THE BONECRUNCHER:
crunches every last morsel!

The Queen invited the BFG in for breakfast

HER MAJESTY

If you had told me that one day I'd meet the Queen of England, I'd have thought you were being very silly indeed!

But then, I don't suppose the Queen was expecting to find ME in her bedroom— or a 24-foot giant in her yard—either. Considering it was the first time the Queen had ever met a giant, she handled it very well indeed.

I couldn't believe it when the BFG thought he'd show the Queen exactly what a whizzpopper was. It sounded like a bomb had gone off in the Great Ballroom, and she nearly jumped out of her skin!

How to Address the Queen (According to the BFG)

Oh, Monacher!

Oh, Golden Sovereign!

Oh, Ruler of Straight Lines!

Oh, Sultana!

I SIMPLY DON'T BELIEVE IT!

The palace clocks made perfect table legs

It was when the Queen found out her subjects were being eaten like popcorn each night that she really came into her own. She really is very good at solving problems.

She summoned the Head of the Army and the Head of the Air Force immediately!

The Head of the Air Force wanted to bomb the brutes, but the Queen said she didn't approve of murder and wanted the giants caught alive.

The BFG found the Queen's breakfast a pleasant change from snozzcumbers

BY GOGGLES!
WHAT DELUNCTIOUS GRUBBLE!

So, of course, it's thanks to her that they are all where they are, at the bottom of a pit.

That means human beans are OFF the menu! I wonder how the giants like snozzcumbers?

THE BFG THINKS THEY'LL FIND THEM DISGUSTEROUS!

Lower him in gently, now!

Matilda

PROUDLY PRESENTING:

Matilda
Your book-loving guide

Mr. and Mrs. Wormwood
Possibly the world's worst parents

Miss Honey
Matilda's sweet and caring teacher

Miss Trunchbull
A beastly headmistress who loathes children

Hortensia
A pupil at Crunchem Primary,
and a brave crusader

Lavender
Matilda's gutsy best friend

Amanda Thripp
A girl who should know better
than to wear pigtails

Bruce Bogtrotter
A heroic boy who can't resist
chocolate cake

Matilda

Books let me escape into exciting worlds

Hello! I'm Matilda. Although I may SEEM perfectly ordinary from the outside, I suppose I am unusual. I could read by the age of three, and by four I always had my nose in a book.

The problem was my parents NEVER noticed me ... They were too busy watching TV. Even when Miss Honey told them I had a brilliant mind, they just laughed.

I know it's wrong to hate your parents, but it's hard not to when the only attention they ever give you is to call you stupid. It made my blood BOIL!

Reading wonderful books like *Great Expectations* by Charles Dickens

Marvelous Tricks

It feels like little sparks of lightning are flashing out of my eyes

As Napoleon once said, the only sensible thing to do when you're attacked is to COUNTER attack. So I began to play all kinds of tricks on my poisonous parents . . .

When I started school and met the beastly headmistress, Miss Trunchbull, I discovered an even better talent . . . I had an extraordinary, MAGICAL power!

ELECTRICITY SEEMS TO FLOW INSIDE MY HEAD.

I simply shouted the words in my head, and the glass moved!

Imagine being able to move something just by staring very hard at it and willing it to happen. It turned out to be very useful.

Meet the Parents

My father, Mr. Wormwood, is a secondhand car salesman. He's also a cheating crook—he thinks customers SHOULD be swindled.

Dad hates me reading: in fact, he once grabbed the library book I was reading and ripped it to shreds.

WHAT'S WRONG WITH THE TV?

MY MOTHER THINKS THAT LOOKS COUNT FOR MORE THAN BOOKS!

As for my mother, her favorite things are watching soppy love dramas and playing bingo. That's why she's so plump—she spends most of her time sitting down.

Mum doesn't hold with clever girls. As she says, "Being brainy won't find you a husband!"

← Another rotten television romance

The Ghostly Parrot

The first trick I played was to put Superglue in Dad's hat. His hair was just starting to grow back when I dreamed up my next trick.

I borrowed a talking parrot from a friend and wedged Chopper's cage up the chimney in our dining room. That evening, a voice rang out, "Hello, hello, hello!"

RATTLE MY BONES!

Mum and Dad were petrified. We crept into the dining room, and then came the ghostly voice again: "Rattle my bones!"

You should have seen Mum and Dad's faces when I told them I'd heard the voice before and the room was DEFINITELY HAUNTED!

RATTLE MY BONES!

Dad right at the back, of course

Bad Hair Day

Always looking in the mirror!

Dad's hair is his pride and joy. He thinks he keeps it in tip-top condition by rubbing Oil of Violets Hair Tonic into it every morning.

One day, he came down for breakfast after his usual routine, and you should have heard Mum's shriek.

You see, I'd simply poured some of Mum's extra-strong blonde hair dye into Dad's hair tonic bottle. His hair went a dreadful dirty-silver shade.

HE THOUGHT HE'D GRABBED THE WRONG BOTTLE BY MISTAKE . . .

Dad's face was priceless when Mum told him it was peroxide, the stuff people use to clean TOILETS!

Miss Honey

She can make a whole class adore her

My teacher, Miss Honey, is everything my parents are not: caring and kind. She never raises her voice.

Miss Honey is the person who recognized that I was talented. She was so convinced of my abilities that she stood up to the Trunchbull—and that takes some courage!

SHE SAID I WAS A GENIUS.

She looks fragile but she's actually incredibly strong

Even when the Trunchbull told her I was nothing but a beastly little worm, she kept believing in me. That's how, together, we overcame the bullies.

Miss Trunchbull

On my first day of school, Miss Honey warned us about the headmistress, Miss Trunchbull. It's best not to get on her bad side!

A neck as thick as a bull's

Fingers like salami sausages

If children get in her way, she just charges straight through them

But it was one of the big girls, Hortensia, who told us how the Trunchbull LOATHES small children. She said we'd be lucky if we survived the first year because the Trunchbull sees the smallest pupils as grubs that have yet to hatch.

I felt sure Hortensia was exaggerating . . . and then I saw the Trunchbull for myself. She looked like an enraged rhinoceros!

The Trunchbull keeping her arm in shape by throwing children

HAMMER THROWING

People have said the Trunchbull looks more like a bloodthirsty hunter than a nice headmistress—but she probably takes that as a compliment!

I bet the Trunchbull thinks, "Why the devil would I want to be nice?" She told us she once threw the hammer for Great Britain at the Olympics, and it wasn't being NICE that got her there.

Oh no, it was being able to bend iron bars and rip phone books in half!

THE TRUNCHBULL WOULD LIKE TO SQUASH US CHILDREN LIKE MAGGOTS.

She loves to hurl an insult much like she throws the hammer—it's got to be fast and it's got to hit the mark. Here are some favorites:

Miserable little gumboil
Nauseating wart
Poisonous pockmark

Calf muscles like grapefruits

Hortensia

I was completely in awe of Hortensia when I first met her. She's 10, and she stands like a giant. Here was someone who had brought the art of misbehavior to perfection!

Hortensia's been in the Trunchbull's torture room, The Chokey, so many times she's lost count. After her first all-day stretch in there, she was bleeding all over!

One time she filled the Trunchbull's gym underwear with itching powder

HORTENSIA SAYS
WE'RE LIKE
AN ARMY
FIGHTING
FOR OUR LIVES!

The Chokey's a tall closet so narrow you can't sit down. You have to stand like a statue the whole time because the walls are covered with broken glass and the door is covered with spiky nails. It's torture!

Lavender

1

2

3

4

5

I met Lavender on the first day of school, and we hit it off right away. She's a skinny little shrimp, but she's plucky!

One morning, Miss Honey mentioned the Trunchbull would be visiting our classroom the next day and someone would have to make sure she had a water pitcher.

Lavender's arm went up like a shot. She was longing to do something heroic.

The Trunchbull shook like Jell-o

LAVENDER HATED THE TRUNCHBULL AS MUCH AS ANY OF US.

I think Lavender felt a bit guilty when Miss Trunchbull ended up blaming me for the newt in her water, but without her gutsy plan, I would never have discovered my incredible power!

Amanda Thripp

I can't say I know Amanda well, but I do know that her mother likes her to look pretty. Wearing pigtails turned out to be a HUGE mistake, though, because if there's one thing the Trunchbull can't abide . . .

HER MOTHER THINKS SHE LOOKS PRETTY WITH PIGTAILS.

What a landing! I bet she was black and blue the next day

I saw Miss Trunchbull coming at Amanda and her pigtails like an enraged bull, and I bet Amanda thought the Day of Judgement had come for sure. The Trunchbull picked her up with one hand and started whirling her around and around with loud grunting noises.

Amanda was screaming blue murder, and then the Trunchbull let go and she went sailing through the air.

Bruce Bogtrotter

Poor Brucie went gray with fear

It's true Bruce is a little plump and really likes to eat, but the Trunchbull was going a bit far when she said he was part of the criminal underworld.

I'm sure Bruce regretted stealing her cake when he realized he was going to have to eat a WHOLE cake— and in front of the entire school.

EAT, EAT, EAT!

But Bruce really got into his stride. Anyone else would have been sick, but not Bogtrotter. He just kept going.

When the last mouthful was gone, you should have seen the Trunchbull's face. Bruce was like a grinning sack of cement. He didn't even notice when she smashed a plate over his head.